In memory of Dr. Hattie Thompson

December 5, 1911 – November 2, 2006

Dedicated to My Grandchildren

Darryl DeWayne Smith, Danielle Kenyatte Justice, Breana Danielle Justice, Tiana Monique Justice, Jamari Najee Johnson, Zaria Shrell Hughes, Bilal Tariq-Madyun, Cameron Jackson, Destini Danielle Slaughter, Elisha Ann Justice, Aaliyah Zahar Tariq-Madyun Shager

Acknowledgement

C. Lewis, Aatiyah Tariq-Madyun, B. Countess Pope, Dr. Hattie Thompson, Brad Cartwright, Canisha Batimba, Lisa Rhode, Jackie Bohannon, Kay Beighley, Laruen Fouse, Dr. Linda Amerson, Dr. Marilyn Lewis Alim, Rachaun Julian, Dr. Mercedes B. Toregano, Robert James, Roxana Alston, Shelby Bray, Tim Knox, Yvonne Edwards, Joyce Barrett, Maria Barberee, Darryl Robinson, Dan Norlander, Maxine Brown and Maggie Breach

Intro to Other Side of the Chair

I decided to write this book because of my love for the industry. I'm often questioned by my colleagues about alternative income streams. I heard about their challenges and I felt there pain. Many of them are supplementing their income outside the industry while others have left altogether. Some feel burned out. The problem is, they have not taken advantage of the other side of the chair. Many of them have been doing hair for some 20 or 25 years, while some have as little as 10 years' experience, but they have something in common; they feel there's something else they could be doing in the industry, but WHAT? This book is the answer to the question of what they can contribute.

My mentor, Dr. Hattie Thompson, once said to me, "People can become rich and have a lifestyle just by practicing trichology. They could make real money and there are people seeking out specialists in hair and scalp disorders. But in order for them to really create wealth in the industry then they need to look at multiple streams of income."

For the first 15 or 20 years of my practice, I've concentrated on training trichologists across this country and beyond, throughout the Caribbean, Canada and as far away as Korea. My main concern was to teach the basics of trichology along with a continuing education arm and then transition into the marketing part.

Thus, my motivation for writing this book is just to give back to an industry that gave so much to me and to my family. I do this by showing some of the ways you can make money on the other side of the chair and create multiple streams of income.

Let's first define the term; trichologist. Trichology is the scientific study of hair and scalp disorders. Around 1902 in London, England, a group of scientists got together and realized there was a correlation between hair and scalp disorders and the body's systems. They created a science called trichology, the word derived from a Greek word for hair (tricho) and ology, which means "the study of". At first, trichology was just the study of hair, but eventually it expanded to the study of scalp disorders as well.

When I began the study in the 1980s it was still considered a para-medical field, but it soon evolved into an alternative medicine field. As we learned more, we realized that even alternative medicine was not really enough for us, and so we began to align ourselves with another branch of medicine called 'Integrated Medicine'. As practitioners we work with both alternative and conventional methods.

One thing to understand is that this practice is like that of a specialist. If you're looking for a General Practitioner then you can go to any place and find one, but if you seek a specialist, you'll be expecting something different. For example if you go to your family practice doctor with a heart problem you will be referred to a Cardiologist. Your GP will not treat heart problems effectively problem. Likewise, cosmologists and barbers will send clients to the Trichologist or Hair Loss Prevention Specialist for problems related to the hair and scalp i.e. scaly scalp, hair breakage, bald spots and patchy baldness.

The target market is those who are making $100,000 a year or those who aspire to be in that realm in the next 12 to 18 months. I've found that some people are really looking just to do what I did when I came out of beauty school, which was to fry it, dye it and lay it to the side. At that stage I, like my colleagues, was not interested in anything with hair or scalp disorders. However, once I was in the industry people began to come to me with hair problems. I began to seek solutions for them. These included all kind of home remedies, such as Glovers Mange Cure and olive oil. Some might work sometimes, but there was nothing reliable. I was sincerely looking for answers.

I went to the school where I had trained; I went to other teachers; I went to other places and the best I could find anywhere was mom and pop remedies. There was never scientific approach to this so I made a decision; I would put together a banquet for the hair care professionals in North Alabama and Southern Tennessee. I found out the names of those had been involved in hair care for the longest and who had contributed most to the industry because I wanted to honor them in a 'This is Your Life' style banquet.

In my search for subjects for my banquet, I met Dr. Hattie Thompson, who had then been in the industry for well over 50 years. She was already in semi-retirement and had a patent on a hair growth product in Washington DC. I went to interview her. At the end of the interview, I said, "What is this trichology stuff?" She said,

"Well that's a hair doctor." "Well I'm a hair doctor," I said. She explained to me the scientific approach to what she was doing and I realized how little I really knew.

I remember my first encounter with one of my clients who said, "I'm having some hair loss; what is my problem?" I gave the universal answer, "I don't know." I happened to be working with a girl who had been in the industry for maybe 15 or 16 years. So one of her clients came in one day with the same problem and I just happened to overhear her response to that same problem. "Well you've got stress." "No I don't," said the client. "Well, are you married?" "Yeah." "You got children?" "Yeah." "You got other pressures?" "Yeah." "You work?" "Yeah." "Then you got stress." And so that was the answer.

So I found the answer to all hair loss problems right there in front of me. Every time a client came in with that problem after that, guess what happened? They had stress. Every client had stress from that point. Because the reality is this, if the only tool you have is a hammer everything looks like a nail. And that's the reality.

That's what I had to deal with for a long time. And then after a while it began to feel as if I was really not being honest with people. It was like when you're plugging your fingers in your ears and you can hear yourself talking; you know something's not right. I began to research the subject, but found nothing of value until I met my mentor and teacher Dr. Hattie Thompson.

Table of Contents

CHAPTER ONE:
Treat Your Business Like a Business

Q: Why do people fail in business?

A: In my 40 plus years in business. I've worked with many different businesses models. I'd like to say that every businesses I owned was a success. However, the truth is I've had more failures than success.

My biggest lessons was from the failures rather than from the successes.

I find that many entrepreneurs fail in business because they don't have a success plan. They go into the forest without a map and they cannot find their way through. It's like shooting yourself in the foot. if you don't have a plan to succeed failure's is almost automatic.

I've gone into many businesses and I see that they have no plan. They do have a good idea. Especially in the hair care industry. Because a person has good skill styling. They think that they should open a salon.

However, they fail to realize that business skills and hairdressing skills are two different things.

They think, "Okay well I can do hair so let me open up a salon. When you start hiring people that takes leadership skills.

I've seen a salon owner turn over five, six, seven stylist in a day. Because the stylist were lacking proper leadership.

I've had a situation like that happen with me personally. I had my manager conspire behind my back and open up a salon. She tried to take my stylist with her. So beware those things do happen in business.

Again businesses fail basically because they lack proper planning. Understanding the importance of having a business plan, could save your business.

Q: Do you see that as happening to a particular ethnic group? Or is that just nonsense?

A: That is just nonsense. However, that's a good question. We think that because we're in a particular ethnic group, that's all we see. In reality it crosses racial lines and gender lines.

It's just a fact that business is not your ability to style hair. Business has to do with understanding it's overall makeup. The whole vision start to finish. That is what a business plan does, it helps give direction to you business.

If you're a good cook that doesn't make you a good business owner. And that doesn't mean you should open up a restaurant. If you're a good stylist doesn't mean you should open up a salon. If you're good at changing tires don't mean you should open a tire shop.

It takes a different set of skills to operate a business. It takes being able to construct a business plan, understand and lead people. How do you get your message to the end consumer. That is where marketing comes in, which is another area that we'll be talking about.

These must be understood and implemented for business to successful. Just recently a client opened up a restaurant. He didn't know anything about restaurants business. He spent X amount of dollars trying to put it together. Wouldn't started out with the basic a business plan.

People say, "Okay what I'll do is I'll give you a nice place. I'll decorate it real nice and I have good food."

You could have the best cook and the best decorated place. If no one knows you exist, what's difference does it make.

Q: What is your business plan?

A: Your business plan is your road map that we talked about earlier. That is what you're going need before going into the forest. Your business plan, is an outline of where you are going. For example, if you are going from Alabama to California. You're going to get yourself a road map to chart your way to California.

If you get in your car and start driving you may end up in New York rather than California. So it's important that you have a map before you go into the forest. That's one of the things that my old man used to say, "Don't wait until you get into forest to try and find a road map. Get the map before you go into the woods."

4

Your business plan is actually your road map. It gives you an idea, a concept about where you are. It keeps you on tract as to where your business is heading

Q: What is your vision for the business?

A: The vision is where you want to be in five years from now. I'll have X amount of clients; I'll have expanded this whole block and I'll have served X amount of stylists. In other words your vision is what gives you the forecast or prognosis of what's ahead of you.

For example, when we opened up our first 24 hour beauty salon. My objective was to work there very, very hard for the first five years. And I did. I worked so hard that people saw me there, morning, and night. They were saying, "This guy, he's always there." They used to come into my salon and say, "You are always here."

My average day was about 18 hours. Even though it was a 24 hour service. Sometimes I would leave 12 or 1 o'clock in the morning. I would get a couple of hours of sleep and be right back there by 5am.

The objective of that I knew that I had to work hard to build my business. I had to be there in order for the business to survive. I was willing to make that sacrifice in order to build the business.

But my vision was, Five years from then I would not have to work that hard. And so five years later, well it was probably less than five years. I was actually out teaching Trichology. When I put that plan in place I had never heard of Trichology. Now the same people would come by and say, "You're never here."

You should have a vision about where it is that you want to take your business. I knew personally I wasn't going to be behind a chair like that for any length of time. My objective was to be, on the other side of the chair.

At the time I knew very little about what I was distant to do. I didn't know anything about Trichology. My mission and my vision was to share my knowledge with other hair care professionals.

Q: Why is your mission part of the business plan?

A: Your mission is your range of activities that you actually focus on in your business. It is what you're doing now. While your vision is what you project to be doing in the future.

They kind of tie hand in hand. Sometimes your mission and your vision can be confusing. But your mission is your focus." Again for us we specialized in hair and scalp disorders. We use for an example today a lot of people specializing in growing your own hair. We were very successful in pioneering the term "hair care specialist."

Q: Where can a good business plan be found?

A: Well interestingly enough I would recommend now go on the internet. But personally when we started off we had a local college that's Business Department would take on X amount of businesses and build business plans for them. And we were just fortunate to have a local University build our first business plan for us and it was very, very successful.

Again I would highly recommend just going on the internet and just put in 'business plan' and see what you come up with. I see one that has 500 different plans that you can just use as an example for yours and then plug the information there and that would be a business plan.

But a business plan again is not static. A business plan, you know you're always expanding on your business plan. What I recommend, I hope I'm not jumping the gun right now, I think I am. Make sure that you go over your business plan.

Again you can find it on the internet; you can go to a public library; often times if you go to a local University that has a Business Department there, you can find some people who develop a business plans for a living.

That would be my recommendation for that. But again mine was by the local University; they did a fantastic job by the way, I don't know if it would be right for me to say that the University is the UAH University of Huntsville in Alabama. But Huntsville, they did an excellent job building my first business plan.

Q: Well you answered number six excellently which was who writes the business plan so we'll just move right ahead.

When and I think this delves right into what you were saying, but it needs to be known, when should a business plan be written?

A: Again a business plan should be written before you open up your business. You should have an idea what it is that you want; how much money do you need in order to run your business, because a business plan gives you A-Z basically for what it is that you're doing; it gives you your rent; your utilities; it tells you your location; it gives you your mission statement; it gives you the whole thing.

So now you have an idea about where it is you want to go. Again you want to go back and look at it.

Make sure that you write the business plan before you go into business that's for sure.

For example, in our business that we had the University wrote our business plan. It was written probably maybe about six months to a year before we ever opened up the business. So we can review it; so you can go over all the information.

It gave us a map and what I did with my first business plan which was designed for my family to go into business with me. Unfortunately that never did happen.

For years I've been trying to get my family to go into business and I said, "Maybe I'm asking them to do too much so let me go and put together the business plan; present the business plan layout to them, what the business plan is and then maybe it would be a little easier to see the concept and come on board."

Unfortunately my immediate biological family was not the ones that came, but I did form a family that actually helped the business to grow and it was a wonderful experience .

Q: Really excellent answers. You also really just answered number nine, which is, is a business plan part of an overall strategy for the business? That's an excellent answer, and so we'll just move to number 10.

Q: Why is marketing a part of the business plan?

A: I find this to be one of the weakest parts, especially for small and medium sized businesses, is the marketing. And the reason why I think this is because it's not really clear how important marketing is for a business.

For example, say I go into a restaurant and they have a very, very good cook. I'm sitting there and I'm eating there and then after the meal is over I say, "Oh my compliments to the cook, bring the cook out so I can give them a special tip." And he comes out and 'cause I tip the cook and I say, "What are you doing working here at this restaurant, you should have your own restaurant as good as you cook?" So he replies, "I hear that all the time."

I come back six months later he's no longer there; he's moved down the street and around the corner and he's opened up his own restaurant. And I go down there and the food is good but the service is terrible. And six months later he's closed down.

Not because he wasn't a good cook but because he didn't really understand the business part of it.

I've seen in the area of marketing someone have a mediocre restaurant but good marketing, become very, very successful. I've seen other owners with excellent skills, very, very good cooks with no marketing fail. Not because of the food, but the other person had the better marketing.

Business owners don't really understand that if your consumers are not aware that you exist and what you're doing, if your message isn't clear to them then you'll end up going out of business. It's unfortunate.

Now I remember one of the stories I tell is that you can rent the Civic Center in your city, you can have the best DJ and you can get the best person to come in there and decorate everything and you can hire the best caterers but if you don't send out any invitations chances are nobody shows up.

So your marketing is your invitation to your end consumer; to your target market to let them know that you're there and that you have what they need; what they want; what they're looking for; you're the provider for that. And that's the key to that particular part, the marketing part. So, so important.

We'll talk about marketing a little later but I just want to kind of touch on that a little bit there.

Q: How often should the business plan be reviewed?

A: A business plan should be reviewed at least once a quarter. And I highly recommend and a start-up business to review your business plan once a month for at least the first 12 months.

Because what happens is that as you go into business you'll see things change because business is not stagnant, it fluctuates. So as a result you have to stay on top of that and your plan again is just like if you're taking again a trip to New York or California, either one, and you're on your way to your destination and you see a detour. You don't stop and turn around and go back where you came from, you just detour around where the detour is and you continue to go on your way to where you're going.

In your business you'll find the same thing; you'll find a detour; you'll find miscellaneous things that you hadn't planned to happen but you don't close your business because of that you just detour around that and continue to grow with your business. And the same with your business plan.

So that would be my recommendation; at least a quarter and initially in a start-up business once a month for at least the first 12 months.

Q: Excellent because I would have thought it would have been once a year, so that's excellent information.

A: I go into some business and I say, "Do you have a business plan?"... and I will tell you right now if I go into 10 salons and ask them for a business plan maybe two out of 10 will have a business plan.

And one out of the two would have looked at their business plan in the last six months. The other one often times have not looked at their business plan since they had it. It's sometimes propping up the door; sometimes it's on the very top shelf collecting dust because we don't understand that a business plan is not just to start your business, but this is your ongoing; something you have to revisit.

If you're driving on the road and you're on your way to a destination you're not looking at the map one time. As you go along that road you're start looking to see, especially if you have to change highways, from one highway to another, you're want to know where you're change from. The same thing in your business plan.

If I'm going to Philadelphia for example, okay I know I take 72 out to 24, 24 to 75, 75 to 81. But as I'm going up there I'm looking back and forth at the map to make sure that I'm making the right turns and I'm transitioning at the right place to go to these places. And the same thing happens with your business plan, go back and look at it again and again as you travel along the road to your success to what your vision is; where you're going.

Q: Will an attorney be needed in the review of the business plan?

A: Not necessarily. It would be good to have them maybe like once a year to go over it, but not necessarily every month or every quarter, it wouldn't be necessary for them to review it that frequently. But it's always good to have an attorney there; an attorney should be one of your team and you can go back and forth with them on the things that you need.

Q: Will an Accountant be needed as a consultant in outlining the finances in the business plan?

A: I would say so. I would definitely recommend that because again this is one of your team members. Every business plan is not for financing. Whether you want financing or not I would recommend the business plan, but it's not necessary for just financing alone.

If your objective of your business plan is to get finance or get investors to invest in your business. Then it becomes necessary because investors want to know, that you know what your plan is?

You can tell them one thing, but they want to see what you have in writing; what it is that you have in writing that you really have thought this out. And a business plan means it's something that you have thought out. Hopefully it means that to you, that you have actually looked at this business.

For example, we have our business plan and we are looking at the possibility of financing and most of my businesses we financed ourselves, but we've had good relationships with attorneys and bankers and accountants in order to make sure that we stay on track; that our taxes and everything are taken care of accordingly.

Q: Why do lenders want access to the business plan?

A: And again because they want to make sure they get their money back; they want to make sure that you have something that's solid and you could show them that, "This is our projections over the next four or five years we plan on doing this," because it's laid out there.

We've just completed a business plan for the Hair Loss Prevention Institute. One of the projections that if we recruit 20 students per month over the next six months. The result in revenue is $350,000.With those projections a loan for $50,000 or $100,000 is doable.

Now one of the other things of course they want to make sure that you have a track record. That you have the experience to make this business work. That is where your business plan shows that you're not just doing this because this is an opportunist. This demonstrates you have some kind of insight and gives credence to your ability to be successful.

It kind of reminds me of the story about the richest man in Babylon. One of the stories talks about a guy, he comes in and he tells this guy, he says, "I understand you're the richest man in Babylon, can you teach me how to be rich?" He says, "Sure." He says, "What I want you to do is save 10% of your money until next year, when I come back we'll invest it."

He starts saving 10% and when his buddy came in about six months later with the best deal ever. He had a deal to purchase precious stones. He nor the buddy knew anything about precious stones. They took the money, the 10%

that he had and they invested it all in precious stones.

So when the rich man returned a year later he said, "Well what happened?" He said, "Well I lost the 10%." He said, "Well you lost it because you were not familiar with, precious stones. The buddy didn't know anything about them and the guy that ripped you all off he did."

That can often times be the situation. If it's something that you don't know anything about don't invest. I've seen it happen personally with one of the guys I was coaching recently. He invested a lot of money in some things that he didn't know anything about and lost it and lost his shirt doing it. So you have to be very, very careful about those things as well.

Q: We were talking about why lenders want access to the business plan?

A: The reason why they look at your business plan is to see a logical and systematic way to make money.

They want you to repay them the money they lend to you.

Q: Okay well let's stay in that same frame of mind. The next question: I'm not seeking a loan; will I still need a business plan?

A: Absolutely you still need a business plan. Whether you're seeking a loan or not you would still need to know what your strengths and weakness, your vision and your marketing strategies are. The business plan outlines all that for you and gives you a clear obvious concept about where it is that you're going.

Q: What is the difference in being in business and being self-employed?

A: Now this is one of the questions that unfortunately many small businesses think that they're in business and they're just self-employed.

Self-employed is basically you have created a job for yourself. In other words if I have to be there every day to make sure that the business run you are I'm self-employed. You've just created a job for yourself and for others.

If you're in business you should be able to walk away. A later year come back and be making more money than you did when you walked away.

I remember in Steven Covey's book - The Seven Habits of Highly Effective People - one of the things he talks about is the business visionary opposed to the business manager. He says that a lot of people who have a business they're just business managers, they're not business owners.

In other words if you're an owner you know how to hire people in order to get the job done, you don't have to do it yourself. Like if Donald Trump has 29 different businesses he's not operating all those businesses, he's hiring the best people in order to have those businesses run properly.

I have to say for myself personally for the 40 something years that I was in business I was just self-employed; I was just self-employed because I had to be there every day in order to make this thing happen. If I wasn't there the business did not operate.

Entrepreneurs confuse being in business and being self-employed. They think that a doctor; for example, or a dentist are in business because they have a practice. But the reality is not necessarily. God forbid, the doctor die and that business is not sold in three to four months it's no longer valid. If his wife or children or whoever takes over cannot have that business sold in that time frame. People will go and they'll find themselves another doctor.

So there's a real big difference between the two. We have to very conscious of that in our practice. The question is do we have to be here every day to make this business operate. If we do we've just created our self a job.

I even see people that have a franchise, like a MacDonald franchise, think they are in business. The same rules apply to a franchise. They have a business if they have a manager that can operate without the owner being there. If the owner have to be there, they're not in business, they're just self-employed.

Q: Okay great answers, good question. Do businesses really plan to fail?

A: No they don't really plan to fail, they simply fail to plan. The real key to a successful business is the plan.

Business owners go into the business without a plan to succeed, then failure is almost guaranteed.

I'm not saying that you can't eke out a living without a plan. I'm not saying that you will not have a store front. They're self-employed and they're making a living, they brought a car and a house. Okay you are making $25,000, $50,000 a year that could be very good. But if you're leaving $200,000 on the table is that still good.

That's the difference between the two, plan and no plan . Okay I'm making a living so I'm okay with this. I just want to buy a house and a car. But how many houses and cars are you leaving on the table at the same time.

The bottom line is businesses don't really plan to fail they just fail to plan.

Q: Why address strengths and weaknesses?

A: That's one of the key elements of a business plan is your strengths and weaknesses. The reason for that is that if you understand what you're weak at you can hire somebody in those areas and you can concentrate on your strong points.

Business people spend too much time on their weak areas. That takes away from the reason they went into business in the first place. Your purpose for being in business is to build a business.

But you can't if you're just taking all that time trying to make your weak points strong. Find someone to do that and stick to your strengths. If I'm not good at the accounting part I'm not trying to be an accountant. I would have to stop doing what I do best in order for me to do that.

I remember when I started studying marketing. I realized that I couldn't be a Trichologist and study marketing. I had to finish one and do the other. It was just impossible for me to do both. I could do both but not at the same time. I had trained thousands or perhaps tens of thousands hair care professionals. I was the go to guy in the industry for trichology. It was time for the next level marketing. Does that make sense?

Q: It makes perfect sense.

A: I see often times people try to do both and then they can't get either one of them done because they're two different disciplines.

That brings back a old saying, "To do two things at once is to do neither one of them well."

Exactly.

Q: Can I write my own business plan?

A: Absolutely you can. I recommend you have someone to look it over . There are templates on the internet that you can just fill I the blanks. However, I would recommend someone who's familiar with business plans look it over and check it out for you.

Q: Do I need an exit strategy?

A: Absolutely. An exit strategy basically means, you have a plan just in case you decide to sell your business. That's what an exit strategy is for.

Whether you decide to sell it or not be prepared. Position yourself in the business where if you want to, you can. You don't necessarily have to sell your business. However, have the strategy in place that you can if it becomes necessary.

And it may not be you, it may be your children or your spouse or partners maybe have to sell it. But always have your business built so it can transition if ever necessary.

CHAPTER TWO:
Outline Your Market Strategy

Q: What is your message?

A: After your business plan marketing is the key to your success. There for your marketing message must be clear to your end consumer.

I use the analogy sometimes that your message to your end consumer has to be concise. For example if I'm writing a personal ad, "African American man looking for African American woman between the ages of 35 and 50, likes to cook; likes walks in the park; do not drink or smoke; good in the kitchen and other rooms."

I have defined my message and exactly who I'm looking for. I have also been exact on who I am not looking for. In other words if you drink and or smoke I'm not interested. If you're 55 or 85 I'm not looking for you. If you're Asian or a Caucasian or whatever else I'm not looking for you. I'm now defining what my message is to my end consumer.

Your marketing should be basically the same clear and concise. Your marketing should be as close as possible to a want ad so people know exactly what they are getting.

One of the things I say I really like is 'truth in advertising'. Do you remember Domino's Pizza when they first came out. They said that, "We'll guarantee you that we'll get you a hot juicy pizza to you in 30 minutes or less or you don't have to pay."

So now that is what we call 'truth in ad'. They never said that, "We're give you the secret recipe from the mother country." They never said anything about deep dish or delicious pizza. They just said, "Hot pizza guaranteed 30 minutes or less."

They were outside of a college campus. The college kids were smoking marijuana and they got the munchies. They can just call and get their pizza delivered in 30 minutes or less. The pizza was not even good at the time when they first started. But who cared, they got it there, hot and on time.

So we call that 'truth in advertisement.' So is your message as clear as it can be to your target market, the better off you are.

Q: What impact does your message have on your clients?

A: The impact again is to let them know exactly who it is that should come. If you are Church's Chicken don't come there for a fish sandwich.

Make sure your market knows you're gearing your business towards them and clearly define what you're selling.

The value and benefit of the offer should be apparent. The market should fully understand what it is that they're gaining in the transaction.

Q: Why are your traits and experience important in establishing a viable business?

A: The traits and experience are important, but it is also crucial that you have a passion for what you're doing.

I was 11 when I was introduced to hair in Philadelphia, PA. I grew up there and a lot of the children in my neighborhood couldn't afford haircuts. My first experience with hair was actually cutting hair on my steps for free. I had a pair of scissors, a comb, a little dish, and some soap.

I didn't care about making money, it was something I was passionate about. It was my gift from GOD that I was sharing. I did it well enough that people began to pay me. I messed up a lot of heads before I got good. In life, you have to be willing to lose a little in order to win.

When I was about five or six years old, my mother would have me scratch her hair. When I was done I would fashion some beautiful coiffeurs on her. I mean I would lay her hair out! She was so pretty when I finished with her.

I didn't understand why she would always comb her hair before going outside. Later in life I realized why. I would see other five year olds doing their mother's hair. They'd put mayonnaise and ketchup in the hair, and say, 'Oh, momma, you're just so pretty.'

I think that at five, my results were probably similar to other five year olds'. She was polite to me, but couldn't wear the hairstyle outside. She always encouraged me, within reason.

That's the basis for what I do. I have a real passion for the hair care industry. I am proud to be a part of such a wonderful career.

My father was also a businessman. A lot of people wouldn't consider what he did legitimate business because he was a bootlegger, but he most definitely was. I probably got the business ambition from him and the passion for hair from my mother.

Q: What specific problems do you solve for your target audience?

A: I would say that one of the primary things I address is how to create multiple streams of income. That's really what this particular mission is about. It's about showing my colleagues that there is the other side of the chair. I show them that there's a wealth of opportunities that exists and they can stay inside of the industry and create their own real wealth.

You can monetize your own unique skills and become extremely wealthy. We're going to talk in detail about how to do that a little later.

Q: This question is similar to number four, but how do you solve these problems?

A: We'll be addressing solutions a little later, also. My mentor said to me, 'You can get rich and you can create yourself a lifestyle by doing hair.' However, real wealth is creating multiple streams of income.

My mentor, Dr. Hattie Thompson, was way ahead of her time. In 1953 she developed a hair growth product and had it patented in Washington, DC that same year. She was a millionaire many times over. She never learned how to drive, but she knew how to grow hair. That was her claim to fame.

She was one of the first to emphasize hair care over hair styling. I guess that's why she was a hair 'care' professional. She opened up a school and sold her own hair products. She purchased property, which she rented out, and she operated a salon, where she often showed movies.

She had multiple streams of income and that would account for her ability to create millions of dollars. She showed me her bank book from the 50s, when she used to deposit $500 a week. You can imagine what kind of money that was at that time!

Q: Yeah, probably about $2,000 a month.

A: Exactly.

Q: Define 'geographic marketing'?

A: Geographic marketing basically involves an area or radius that surrounds a business.

For example, a client calls me and says, 'Can you help me with my marketing?' Let's say it's a young man who has just opened a salon and he wants to do some geographic marketing. I would map it out. I would circle a 10 block radius from his location and say, 'This is your geographic marketing area. Blanket this area with your offer.'

The people within this 10 blocks will come and support you. What marketing does is let your prospects know that you and your product or service exist. I'm not saying other people on the other side of town will not support you. If your offer is appealing enough, some clients will drive all the way over from the other side of town for it. I've done that myself many times.

The reality is patrons in your area will support you if they know you're there. This may sometimes be because of convenience only, but it's still a reason, so you want to let people know your business is there. You can do this by posting and handing out flyers or offering value packs to those in your geographical marketing area.

I would recommend that you send out coupons or something similar to let them know you're there. You can offer a buy one get one free, a buy one get half off or come in Tuesdays, a slow time, and get half off.

When I opened my first salon in Madison, Alabama, we used to walk around the neighborhood one day a week shaking hands, passing out flyers and telling people about our services.

That was very effective, especially when we first got started.

Q: Define 'demographic marketing'?

A: With demographic marketing, you want to know as much about your prospect as possible. The demographic would include age, gender, income, education, renters or home owners, etc. You want to talk to people who are 25 to 45, you want to talk to people who have a college education, you want to talk to people who have a 50,000 -$200,000 income. You want to talk to home owners.

That's your demographic. It tells you details about this person, down to what magazines they read. Even, if at all possible, what cereals they eat. You want to know as much about them as you can for demographic marketing.

Q: Define 'affinity marketing'?

A: Affinity marketing involves the associations that you are involved in. For example, if you go to church those people are your 'affinity market.' They have something in common with you.

If you belong to a civic organization, if you play softball, if you belong to the NAACP or an organization like that, or if you have twins and you belong to some group about having twins, these groups can all be a part of your affinity marketing.

Affinity has to do with the commonalities you have with others who belong to the same associations and organizations that you do.

Q: Why are past and present clients the most overlooked?

A: That's an issue I find very problematic. I imagine marketing to be about always trying to get new customers. I used to have very little reason to contact past and present customers.

I go to salons and hair clinics now and I ask about the past and present customers. We tend to always try to get more new customers without really satisfying the ones that we already have. Big mistake, very big mistake

The reality is that we don't have anything new to market to them.

Every month businesses offer some sort of new marketing for their customers. For example, in January they have Martin Luther King Day; in February they have President's Day; in March they have March Madness; in

April they have Easter; in May they have Mother's Day; June, Father's Day. There's always a sale going on during these times that give offers to past and present customers.

Small businesses often overlook creating new offers. For example, in the salon industry, if you have no coupons, discounts or special offers, why should you contact a business? Once these incentives are created, you have a reason to contact past and present customers.

Some businesses advertise, 'When you come in bring your mother, father, sister or brother, you get half price or free.' When you add something FREE that always works.

You might switch it up every month. The next month you discount hair color prices. The following month you slash haircuts, half price. The next month perms, half price. Remember that marketing is the ability to offer value to your target market. Whatever your business, add something of value and you can always go back to those clients. But, most small businesses don't understand the effectiveness of going back to your past and present customers.

Q: When should word-of-mouth advertising be used?

A: I ask a lot of business owners, 'Are you doing any marketing?' And their response is often, 'No. I'm just using word-of-mouth advertising.' 'How are you doing word-of-mouth advertising when you just opened up your business a month ago, or six months ago? Who knows about you to give word-of-mouth?' My mentor, Mr. Hundley Batts, said 'Word of mouth can hurt you.'

Word-of-mouth advertisement is good if you're already established. But, it is not reliable if you're not established.

I was talking to one of my coaching clients the other day. I said the same thing to them, 'Word of mouth marketing can make or break you. If the wrong words get out there, that can break you. Be very careful about the word of mouth advertisement.'

After you're established and want to try word-of-mouth advertisements, okay. But, if word-of-mouth advertisements were so good then McDonald's wouldn't spend millions a year on advertising.

Q: Makes sense. What about email marketing?

A: Email marketing has proven to be very effective and economic. Small businesses tend to not create databases. They don't understand the importance of keeping in contact with their past and present customers.

A customer comes in, buys whatever he or she wants and leaves. They don't have any way to contact that customer until the next time they come in.

Create a database for your color customer. When you run a special on color contact them. You can email them and say, 'Look, we're having a special on color this month.'

Understand that once you create a database that becomes your asset. In business we talk about two things, assets and liabilities. Often we don't understand the difference between an asset and a liability. The best example I have ever read was Robert Kiyosaki's book *Rich Dad, Poor Dad.*

If you have an asset, it will put money in your pocket. Liabilities take money out of your pocket.

So your customer database is your asset. If you create a large enough asset, you can almost write money at will. Now I give the analogy with John Lennon, one of the Beatles. When John Lennon decided to buy himself a new house, he said, 'I'm going to write myself a new house.' He knew if he wrote a song that he could buy himself a new house.

Once you understand the importance of a database, you can write money at will.

Q: Where do I get an email list?

A: There are some email lists that you can buy. One good source is Reference USA, you can buy lists from them. You can call a list broker, they have lists for sale. You can take the time to build yourself a personal list using Facebook. You can contact people on other social media platforms to build your lists as well.

Q: How can marketing via Facebook become a positive marketing tool?

A: You can use Facebook to create the database I mentioned earlier. Initially they didn't do any marketing, but now they're one of the major marketing tools that we can use.

It's called 'Facebook marketing' but actually it's marketing through Facebook. Even though the principles of marketing have not changed, the tools that we use to market with have. Marketing principles will remain the same. You create your message, identify your market, and find an affordable way to reach them.

Your marketing is offering solutions to your target market. You ask yourself, 'What is it that's keeping them up at night?' Your solution offers a better night's sleep. That's what marketing does.

Q: Can Twitter be a marketing tool?

A: Yes. Twitter, Facebook, all those social media outlets now have positioned themselves to be able to become very effective marketing tools.

Q: Can Instagram marketing be used effectively?

A: Absolutely. Instagram is a social media site that makes photographs. They're also able to do messaging as well. They are now getting a reputation as one of the major marketers in social media.

Q: Why do many small businesses under-utilize marketing techniques?

A: I would say most of the small businesses under-utilize marketing techniques because they don't really understand the importance of marketing.

Let's say, for example, I walk into a store and I'm talking to the proprietor. I say to them, 'What kind of marketing do you use?' They reply, 'We don't use any marketing.' So I respond, 'Why?' 'Because we used marketing and it wasn't effective for us.' 'Okay, what do you mean?' 'I advertised on some radio station for six months and I didn't see any results.'

You may not see the results for a year from now for marketing you're doing right now. That's why marketing, like investing, is an ongoing process. It's something that you do consistently, it is not a stop and go process. You continue to do it until it pays off for you.

You don't see McDonald's marketing sometimes, then not at all. They're always marketing. Every time they're associated with a movie that's being released, they have a new toy to go with it. They have a special on the McRib. Now they have a premium coffee. Watch out Starbucks. They're always running marketing campaigns.

But small businesses tend not to understand that it's not the product as much as the marketing. Stylist think the product they have or the service that they provide makes the difference. They think, 'I can do some good hair,' that should be enough. It's not enough because you're being good doesn't cut it if nobody knows about it.

Your marketing is the ability to let your target audience know that you're good. You could be the best in the world, but if no one knows about you you'll probably end up broke.

Q: How can radio marketing command the attention of listeners?

A: One of the benefits of radio marketing is that you can go to the station and find out what the demographics are. You know if they're serving the hip hop, classic or country western audience. You can know if they're serving renters or homeowners.

You can find out the market that's listening to them, and choose the radio marketing vehicle that's best for you.

Q: How can print ads be made more appealing to the eye?

A: Print ads can add colors and size to an otherwise dull display. Also, with print ads you have what's called 'white space' and you don't want it to look too cluttered. You want to make sure the information is clear to the potential customer.

I remember doing Yellow Pages ads and trying to fit everything in that little space. The account executive said, 'You'll have too much clutter. People get lost when the ad is too busy.

The less clutter you have the more attention your ad gets.'

You want to make sure that you have what we call 'response ads.' This is how you know when someone has read your ad. Sometimes small businesses don't realize that they need a response to their advertising and marketing.

Small businesses don't have a lot of money to spend on marketing. If you have response ads or if you just use emails, you need to be able to calculate your response rate. You may send out 10 emails a day or 20 or 10. Your email might state, 'If you respond to this email, you get a free hair cut.' When your potential clients respond back, then you know how your marketing is working. Remember to always include an expiration date on your offers.

Then, if that's working for you, you can spend more time and money on that campaign.

Q: What does TV marketing add to your business?

A: TV marketing makes it harder to target your market, because even if you choose Spike TV, the fact that men are watching will increase your chances of reaching your target market.

When you start talking about using television for advertising, I would say you have to spend somewhere between $6,000-$10,000 a month. Television marketing is very expensive. I recommend direct response in order for you to be successful.

Q: When should billboards be used?

A: I would use a billboard as a top tier program. Like television, I would use a direct response format.

In other words, no one is going to read a whole billboard at a traffic light. However, you direct them to go to your website. That's one way to use a billboard.

If someone said to me, 'I want to use a billboard,' I would respond, "Use the billboard as a direct response tool.' What's most important is that you get some kind of response.

Q: What about direct mail?

A: Your direct mail is probably one of the most powerful tools that a marketer can use. Lots of people say, 'Well, direct mail is dying because you've got social media now, you've got the internet.'

If you still see those letters in your mailbox that have advertisements, that's what we call direct mail. It is still alive and kicking. It is quite effective. Millions and millions of dollars are spent every year on direct mail, so we know that it's still a very vibrant way of marketing.

I first started studying marketing a few years ago. I went to a library and looked through magazines. I researched my industry's advertisements, then cut them out or copied them. I created what is called a 'swipe file' with that information. I then had millions of dollars worth of marketing material.

You take the time to study those ads that have cost millions of dollars. Learn from the material in your swipe file and write your own copy from that. That's called 'ad copy.'

In one of the study's that Dan Kennedy did, a guy sent one page out and got a response. Every time he sent out more, and he sent as many as 64 pages out, the number of his responses increased.

CHAPTER THREE:
Business Is A Team Sport

Q: How about having a mentor/coach as a guide?

A: I would say you absolutely should. I was not successful in business until I found a coach/mentor. I studied success across many occupations; the most successful people always have coaches/mentors. Whether that's on a basketball team, baseball team, Olympic team, business, whatever it is, a coach/mentor was always key.

A coach/mentor shares, inspires, and motivates you to accomplish your goals, so it's well worth having one.

I know I couldn't be where I am today without the mentors I have in my life. I never find myself in a position where I'm without a mentor.. I can always bounce ideas off of them, asking, 'What do you think about this?' You just can't do everything by yourself, especially in business because it's a team sport.

If you try to do it by yourself, your competition is always going to win. Why? Because they understand the importance of having a team. It's just like in a football game. If you're the only man on your team, you have no chance of winning because your opponent has a whole team.

Always have a team that's led by you and supported by your coach/mentor.

Q: The second team member's an attorney?

A: Absolutely. Again, if you're in business you're going to have a lot of legal issues that you'll have to deal with. If you're a small business, you may not ever go into selling, but you will always have the opportunity to have a start-up. If you lease a building, your attorney will make sure the lease is in order.

If someone comes into your business and suffers a personal injury, make sure you have an attorney to handle that situation.

If you decide you don't want to lease and you'd rather buy, have your attorney instruct you about real estate. If you're building an addition to your business, confirm the construction permits with your attorney.

I would always recommend that you have an entity, LLC or corporation. This will protect you from personal liabilities. The entity is personally responsible for any business losses. Without the proper entity in place, you could lose everything.

One of the things I want to mention about having an attorney and corporation is that you want to be able to position yourself so that your business is an Incorporation. You should also have another corporation that's a Holding Corporation for your business.

In other words, your business shouldn't *own* anything. Your business should be leasing all of its equipment and everything from your Holding Corporation. This should be the entity that owns everything; your business itself shouldn't own anything.

If somebody sues your business, they can't get any of your equipment or anything else because you don't own anything, just lease through your Holding Corporation.

The original purpose of corporations was to protect personal assets as opposed to business assets. Americans would travel via ship to other places to buy things. They would buy coffee or other products. If the ship sank and all the people on board drowned, the entity bore the burden. However, if you did not have an entity, you were personally responsible for the men on board.

When your business grows and you consider mergers and acquisitions for financing, you must have an attorney. Also, if you are involved in sales of assets and stocks, you have to have an attorney.

Again, when it comes to team building my message is the same as the one I got from Robert Kiyosaki. He said, 'If you're the smartest person on your team, you don't need the team. If you're smarter than your attorney, that's not the attorney for you. You need an attorney that's smarter than you, one that can help you and direct you. If you're smarter than they are, you don't need them.'

Always have people on your team who are smarter than you are.

Does that make sense?

Q: That makes a whole lot of sense to me. Our next team member, a banker?

A: Banker. Again, if you're going to be borrowing money, you need a relationship with a banker. Even if you are not, I always recommend having a good relationship with your banker. They will share information with you about what's new in their industry, like giving you the latest info about lines of credit or even how to have different accounts. I highly recommend having a banker on your team.

Q: What's the importance of having an accountant?

A: Man, now you're talking. One of my business plans was developed by my accountant. I can't really begin to express how important an accountant is for your team. They make sure you're doing your taxes, they make sure all your business is in proper order.

Small businesses start off paying payroll out of their pockets. I highly recommend that they find a company to take care of their payroll. Accountants can handle that for you. I see a lot of businesses paying their employees cash money out of their pockets.

Sometimes we go into businesses, paying people under the table. We think that's the wise thing to do, but that's not always the case. If someone you're paying under the table gets upset with you, they can report you to the IRS. Then you may find yourself in a lot of trouble because you haven't really been abiding tax laws.

If this is your friend and you want to give them money, just give them money, without compromising your business.

Something I often tell small businesses is, 'Don't let your small business make you small minded.' I stole that from Brandon Burchard. Always think of your business as a big business.

Having an open mind means you should see why you need an accountant on your team.

Q: What about insurance?

A: This is one of the most important aspects of your business. Imagine everything's going well and someone enters your business and trips and falls. Without having the proper insurance, you could be out of business the next day.

Make sure you're covered. I think they call that CYA, 'Cover Your Assets.'

Q: What about taxes?

A: One of the good things about being in business is that taxes are taken out after expenses. With payroll taxes, when you get your money, the taxes are already taken out. For a business, after you pay your expenses, you pay taxes on what's left over.

Taxes are much different for an individual than a business. I would recommend that you have someone that specializes in taxes on your team.

Q: What about contracts?

A: Make sure your attorney looks them over. Sometimes businesses have internal contracts that you use within your business. They outline your hiring practices and point out the expectations you have of employees. Other contracts may concern business outside of your internal affairs.

Make sure these things are taken care of in perfect order. This is not a personal matter, this is business.

When I hired my brother, he just didn't treat the business like business. He treated the business like it was a hobby. I had to confront him on several occasions, and had to eventually fire him. Firing him wasn't easy, but after doing that, it was easier to fire other employees.

Make sure your contracts are in order and that your business is yours, in name and practice.

Q: What about a biologist?

A: When you specialize in the hair care industry, a biologist is very important. We study hair and scalp disorders, so a biologist will always come in handy, if for nothing more than to bounce ideas off of.

I always had a biologist on my team. I could always go to them to ask questions when particular problems arose.

Q: What about security?

A: I'm fortunate that after having several different businesses, I've never had a break in. I've always had pretty good security. I've had security systems and, in certain cases, even had security guards to make sure the business was protected.

I highly recommend security for your business. Some people say, "Well, if you're not in a bad neighborhood..." It doesn't matter whether you're in a good or bad neighborhood. You still need it.

For several years, I worked 65 miles from my house, at a clinic. Sometimes it took me about an hour and 15 minutes to get to work, because I had to go through a lot of small towns where the speed limits were 30-35 miles an hour.

I remember being at home and getting a call from my security saying that the alarm just went off. Sometimes I had to drive 65 miles back home to turn off the alarm. Sometimes security would cut it off. Other times I had colleagues who lived close and had keys check it out.

Security is important, I highly recommend it.

Q: How about an MD, medical doctor?

A: Absolutely. Again, in the field of trichology, and even in cosmetology, I would highly recommend having a medical doctor on your team. If you're having problems, the advice of a medical doctor can be invaluable.

The field started off as a para-medical field and grew into an integrated medicine field. There's a real need to stay close with the medical industry.

Q: How about an endocrinologist?

A: Very important. After hereditary hair loss, the endocrine system ranks next in line. This system secretes hormones directly into the blood stream. Too much or too little can lead to hair loss. So, an endocrinologist would be someone who we would work hand-in-hand with, sending clients who are having hormonal imbalances to the endocrinologist.

Q: How about intellectual property?

A: You should have an attorney who specializes in intellectual property. If you are creating information products, without the proper protection, people can rip you off.

Make sure that you're covered in that particular area. A lot of the information that we work with is intellectual property. Much of the research and discovery results are intellectual property. So, make sure you have someone to help you protect that info.

Q: How about a dentist?

A: A lot of people don't realize that hair loss can be directly related to problems with dentistry.

For example, one of the problems we see is silver fillings. The mercury in silver fillings is toxic to the body. A result of that toxicity can be hair loss. We're looking for different areas now to identify the causes of hair loss. The problem sometimes is silver fillings.

Sometimes you can see a septic infection in the mouth. This can also cause hair loss. A dentist would know how to deal with this.

Q: What about a dermatologist?

A: In our industry, if a person seems to have a scalp, hair or skin problem, it's our practice to send them to the dermatologist. They are a necessary part of our team, but we don't exclusively work with them.

Q: What about a psychologist?

A: Absolutely. There's a particular disorder that we deal with called trichotillomania, which is a disorder where people actually pull or pluck hair from different parts of their body. Sometimes from their head; I've seen some people do it from the navel area; sometimes from the chest.

This is a nervous disorder. In our small city, we have as many as six or seven different support groups that actually help people who have this particular disorder.

It's hard for you to say to someone, 'You need to see a psychiatrist.' But, sometimes it's necessary to let them know, 'You're problem is trichotillomania and I can recommend a psychiatrist.' You can always recommend a support group.

Q: How important is credit?

A: It's very important. As a business, we have good credit or the ability to repair our credit. We must be in a position to borrow money if we need to. Credit repair or credit restoration are often the best services to use to get in this position if you don't already have good credit.

Q: How necessary is a cosmetologist?

A: We make sure that we keep in contact with other hair care professionals, because some specialize in different areas. At one time, maybe 10 or 15 years ago, stylists tried to do everything themselves. Now we're starting to compartmentalize and cosmetologists are becoming specialists.

You go to an upscale salon or clinic and see a trichologist first. If you go in specifically for a haircut, your next stop would be a barber or stylist, then the shampoo tech, then back to your barber/stylist for your haircut and finish.

In other words, each part is a different department. If you're specializing in one service, you may have to send your client to another department, depending on what they need.

I find that most clients are okay with this process, but some aren't. I offer to send them to someone else more qualified, someone capable of taking care of their needs.

Q: How necessary is a surgeon?

A: When we talk about hair replacement, we're talking about surgery. You need a qualified surgeon that can perform hair replacement services. Hair replacement surgery is having ever-increasing popularity among baby boomers.

Q:What about mergers and acquisitions?

A:This is something an attorney would have to handle. I think we talked about this earlier.

Q: How about the handling of sales of assets and stocks? Who handles that?

A: The attorney. Think we covered this a little earlier, too.

CHAPTER FOUR:
Set Yourself Apart As A Specialist

Q: How should a consultant dress to impress the client?

A: Most stylists tend to look like the average person you might see on the street. What has happened to professional attire? This is one reason we are not considered professional or paid as well as one. Seems people think it's okay to wear anything behind the chair.

I have to take my hat off to the schools, they have maintained the highest standards of excellence, including in regards to attire.

Without maintaining these high standards in the field, we cannot request the type of money that a specialist should command.

However, what seems to be common are dirty capes and jeans; it just doesn't look professional. This look makes the environment seem unprofessional, too. When you start to look like six figures and act like six figures, then, and only then, will you make six figures.

Ask yourself this question. If your doctor dressed in his/her street clothes, would you take them seriously? Would you really want to pay them top dollar?

I expect them to look a certain way. I go there and spend my hard-earned money, I'm expecting them to have a certain dress code.

When I mention dress code in the average salon today, stylists look at me like I am crazy.

I go in salons all the time. I'm often disappointed with how stylists are dressed. They look like they just walked in off the street and started doing hair.

If you want to be average, this book is not for you. It's for those making or aspiring to make six figures plus. When you talk about charging top dollar for what you're doing, at least look like you're worth it.

Q: How does scheduling set the tone for the business?

A: Scheduling is very important. Often I see a client who's scheduled for a 5 o'clock appointment get there at five minutes to five.

The stylist doesn't see them until five minutes after six.

Your clients may put up with that for a little while, but they'll soon be looking elsewhere, no matter how good you are. They'll look for a place that actually cares about them and will abide by their scheduled appointment. This is especially true if you're charging top dollar for your services.

There was a salon in Philadelphia, I don't remember the name, but Patti LaBelle had a boutique in the front. If you were late, they wouldn't let the next customer suffer because you weren't on time.

They had high standards and the highest quality of products; they were very professional. They ran a tight ship because of how well they kept their scheduling.

Q: What creates a pleasant environment?

A: Your environment should be, at the very least, clean. I'm sure that clients don't want to pay someone top dollar for a service and have to clean up the area they're in. The low standards of some salons amazes me.

If you're charging top dollar, make sure that your environment reflects that as well.

Sometimes when you go to a salon, you don't even want to sit down in the place because it doesn't look clean. Cleanliness is so important when people are paying top dollar.

If you're planning on making $100,000 plus a year, then make sure your place looks like that as well. Have a clean place for your clients to go into.

Q: Why are clients willing to ask a specialist for advice?

A: Well, I think that clients are researching the various choices they have. They have an acronym for it; it has to do with on the spot marketing. Back in the day, they would go from store to store to compare prices. Now they can go to one store and check out another store's prices on their cellphone. They can compare prices at point of purchase.

The same thing applies to hair care services. Salon prices can be compared in this same fashion.

They are asking people for advice because they want to be careful with their **spending.** They may be having some problems at home, but they still trust you. You've become like a trusted advisor to them. They're willing to share some things with you that they wouldn't share with anyone else. You're their confidante while you are doing their hair. They may say, 'What do you think about so and so?' They will confide in you like you're their trusted advisor.

Q: Why are proper forms necessary?

A: Proper forms are necessary for you to get the correct information you're seeking. Your forms should represent what it is that you do.

Let's say, for example, you go to a restaurant that sells steak and you get a menu about fish. You would be confused, right?

Your forms have to represent what it is that you do. Our forms are very detailed. We have to know what kind of medication you're taking and how much. Is the medication itself causing the problem that you may be experiencing?

The form itself will give you that kind of information. With the right form you can get the right information often times.

Q: How important is proper equipment?

A: If the only tool you have is a hammer, everything else looks like a nail. Make sure that if you're offering treatments that you have the right tools to perform those treatments.

If you offer laser, steam or some other kind of treatment, the tools are very important. I've seen people try to use products that had nothing to do with their client's request or disorder. I've even seen clients leave because the stylist didn't have the proper tools.

The tools are very important in order for you to accomplish your mission.

Q: How might a co-worker or co-workers enhance the business?

A: We work as a team and that's what helps our business flow. People do not have to sit there waiting for hours to get service. If I'm working on a client and a little behind, my co-worker may prep the client for me or vice versa. It's all about team work and clients like that.

We work as a team in order for us to be successful in business.

Sometimes, and especially with a new stylist, they feel as though they are being neglected. But, what happens is that client may end up being the new stylist's client. That's how I ran my business. I helped to give all my stylists' business.

I know that some stylists say, 'You have all the business, but we don't have that much.' What they don't realize is that my objective was to build the business for them. While they're prepping clients, I can say to a client, 'That the new stylist is really good. '

Q: Is a professional association beneficial?

A: Absolutely. One of the most important factors is it helps to solidify your **credibility** as a professional.

I've always belonged to several different organizations, including the National Cosmetology Association and the Natural

Beauty Culture League. In addition, I was listed in *Who's Who* twice as an executive.

Organizations help to establish you as a professional, too. If you're not a member of one yet, I highly recommend you join one. Check out some local organizations and see exactly what it is that they offer.

Q: Are continuing education classes important?

A: I am a strong advocate of continuing education. It keeps you in the loop of all the latest techniques and updates. Some stylists go to many classes but still can't grow their businesses. This is because they don't understand the value of their business. If you don't see the value in yourself, your clients won't either. The result is you don't increase your price, because you think, 'If I increase my price by even $5, my clients will leave me.'

No, everybody will not leave you. You'll increase your price and some will leave. You'll have fewer clients, but be making more money.

Look at it this way. Would you like to do one person for $400 or 10 for $40 a piece? When you raise your price, somebody is going to leave, but new clients will replace them.

Say, for example, as a coach I charge $150 an hour. When I charged $20 an hour, I had to work twice as hard with a higher volume of clients who were complaining all the time. When I raised my prices, I attracted a different caliber of people; they paid, they had fewer complaints.

As you grow, you're going to leave some clients behind, but that's OK. That's the price of growing a business.

Q: Are today's clients educated?

A: I think we talked about the role of social media and other forms media with today's consumers. We want to make sure that our clients are well educated about the value that we offer. Once they understand your value and see you as their trusted advisor, then you've got a client for life.

Keep your clients educated because that way they understand what it is you're doing. When they see you going to class and see you continuing to grow as a professional, they trust you with their hair or scalp. They trust you as a specialist and happy to pay you what you are worth.

Q: What's the importance of projecting a positive image?

A: When I'm advising business owners, I make them aware that their co-workers may not always agree with them. It's your position as the boss not to become emotional, however, business owners tend to become emotional with their workers.

As Jesus said, 'Turn the other cheek.' In other words, don't let people make you compromise your position because they compromise theirs. You have to stick to who you are in all circumstances. Keep a cool head at all costs. You are in charge when you remain this way.

It's almost like a parent and child relationship. The child may be upset with the parent, but the parent is still in charge. The parent is still responsible for that child. As the business owner, your employees may not always like what you do, they might not even like you.

But, they're your employees and you still have to treat them fairly as long as they're working for you. They are your responsibility no matter how they feel about you. They can like your or dislike you, your job is to treat them all fairly.

You treat them equally and when a problem arises, you can confront them about it. If they get upset with you, that's their problem, not yours.

What you have to do is you have to continue to be the boss and be responsible for everybody who works for you. That's how I try to deal with that particular situation.

Q: Should you showcase your certification?

A: You should have it framed and tacked up on the wall. Frame it and put it in a nice position. The certificate is sort of like a diamond in the rough. A diamond in the rough doesn't look like a diamond. It looks like a charred piece of coal until it's cut and placed in its proper setting. That's when it begins to look like a diamond.

Your certifications can look the same way (like a diamond) when you put them in the proper setting.

Q: Should you make your competition into your comrades?

A: Send your overflow of customers to coworkers or stylists in other salons. Sometimes you may have a client you don't get along with. Maybe your personalities don't click. They might request a service that neither you nor anyone else in your facility can provide, but you know a stylist who provides that service and does it well. I'd say, 'Go to Don, he is very good at that service.'

Once you start sending clients their way, your competition develops a positive attitude towards you. They see you as a comrade, not as a competitor.

Q: Should you make clear the services you provide?

A: There are a couple of ways to do this. It's like writing a personal ad. You make sure you explain what clients you want and the ones you don't want. If a client says, 'I'd like to have this particular style,' your reply should be, 'I'm not a stylist. If you want a stylist, I can recommend one for you. I specialize in hair and scalp disorders. These are the services I offer.' Make that clear to them.

If they want that particular service that you don't provide, recommend a fellow stylist to them. Say to them, 'I specialize in these services exclusively. If you're having hair loss, scalp problems, or scaling problems, I can help you. These are the things that I specialize in.'

This policy can also apply to cuts, color, or permanent waves.

Q: What are the advantageous of owning your own business?

A: I'll also include the disadvantages. The advantage, of course, is that you can set the rules. When you own your business, you set the rules, times, and choose the services you provide.

If expectations aren't made clear from the beginning, workers do what they think is correct. As the owner you expect your staff to act, dress, and perform a certain way. It is your responsibility to tell them that.

You expect that because they graduated from school they'll know what to do. Wrong. If you are a computer specialist with Dell and you go to work for IBM, you're going to take IBM's training. Even though you were already doing the same job or something similar with Dell. IBM wants to make sure that you understand what their training system is. The same thing applies in the hair care industry.

As a business owner, do not just assume that the stylists know your system or expectations. You're in the position now to train them the way you want them to be trained. If a new receptionist came to work for you, even though she was working at XYZ clinical salon before, you would still train her.

At her previous job, she picked up the phone and said, 'Hi. How you doing? This is XYZ salon.' When she comes to your place you may have a different way for her to say the greeting. Your training may be 'We're having a great day at Darryl's High Fashion Salon.' Or, 'We're having an excellent day,' or 'Welcome to Darryl's.'

As the owner you set the stage. That's what you get. You have the advantage of actually setting the stage for what it is that you want your business to ultimately represent.

CHAPTER FIVE Five:
Multiple Streams of Income

Q: What's the importance of consultation?

A: Actually you can build an entire business off of consultations alone. Say for example you charge $125-$225 for a consultation. If you are in a high traffic salon and you administer 10 consultations a day, you've had a good day.

A consultation should be done on every client before any service is conducted. Every high-end salon should make this a prerequisite to insure the integrity of the client's hair beforehand.

Consultations alone could be a very easy career alternative.

Many patrons think consultations and examinations are the same. They are not. A consultation is sitting down with your client going over the form, step-by-step. The person comes in. They fill out a consultation form. Sometimes you don't even see the client. You see the consultation form before you ever see the client.

When you get the consultation form you go through it. You make little checkmarks on it. Make sure you go over with the client because clients overlook small details. When you sit down together, you'll point out information that they didn't notice. That gives you a better idea of how to move forward.

Q: Should you do an examination? How is it different from a consultation?

A: The next step is the examination. You may or may not do the examination the same day as the consultation. Examinations can be done separately, it depends on you. Some practitioners charge $125-$200 for the examination. This is where you're actually going through the hair, looking at bald spots. You are looking at the hair loss and scales that form on the hair and scalp .

That's not necessarily a consultation. The examination is actually hands on. So, the hands on part can be done on a separate follow up. You can separate the two and charge for the consultation and change for the examination.

Q: What's a microscopic analysis?

A: This is where you actually take the hair and look at the integrity of it under the microscope. The microscopic analysis can tell us if the hair is swollen, broken, or fractured. The condition the hair can also reveal different disorders and diseases. This is often referred to as seeing if the hair is 'compromised.'

Q: Does it help to be a TV talk show host?

A: They have a program on now. I can't think of the name of this stylist. She does a TV talk show about hair salons. For stylists with a vision, the opportunities are wide open for shows like these.

You can do it on cable television. Of course you can also do it on a YouTube channel. You can broadcast over YouTube and show exactly what services you provide.

You can interview people just like it's a regular talk show. You can let people know what things you have available.

The challenge then becomes how do you make money off of it? If you're doing a television talk show, you make money from your advertisers. That's how you're making money, or you can actually feature different products every week. The product manufacturer will then pay you to talk about their particular products.

You can interview different hair care professionals or different people from the industry during the television talk show as well.

Q: Is it beneficial to be a radio talk show host?

A: I have personal experience with this because I've had radio talk shows on two separate occasions. We actually had a talk show called *Beauty Shop Talk* and it was very good.

I currently know one particular world class radio talk show host, Dr. Linda Amerson. She does a talk show in Arlington, Texas. I'm a regular contributor on her show. There's a lot of money to be made as a talk show host and you build credibility at the same time.

Again, the money is made in your sponsorship. You can begin to build yourself a database that can help you as well.

If you want to do a talk show, contact the radio station and find out exactly how much money it will cost. That way you know what you need as far as sponsors to be successful.

Q: What is mineral analysis?

A: This is where we actually take the hair and send it to a laboratory that has about $70 million worth of equipment. There the hair is turned into its minerals content. This reveals the excesses or deficiency of minerals in the body.

Hair is a good barometer of what's going on internally in the body. You can take the hair and send it off to the lab and receive a computer printout. It tells you all the excesses and deficiencies, as well as what these could possibly mean.

One of the things we find in Alzheimer's patients is that they have a large amount of aluminum in their hair, which reflects what is going on in the body. However, there is nothing definitive tying aluminum to the cause of Alzheimer's.

Cookware and antiperspirants have a direct correlation to high levels of aluminum. We do know that aluminum cookware and antiperspirants can end up in the body system.

Mineral analysis will help you determine that, as well as how to rectify that particular situation.

Normally you take the hair from the nape area, just below the occipital. You send the hair to us and we send it to the lab. Once that is completed we help you to understand the process and set up your own account. Don't take any more than an inch of hair from the scalp. We want to get the hair closest to the scalp and no more than an inch.

Anything beyond that we just cut it off and discard it. So, if the hair is 10 inches long, we don't really need all of that. We just need an inch.

We have a little scale we use to measure the amount of hair. You submit that information to us and it comes back from the lab with a full printout that reveals the excesses and/or deficiencies. If they have a zinc deficiency and you have a zinc supplement, you can sell them to your client.

One of the things you will learn is that vitamins and minerals work hand-in-hand together, they activate each other. You shouldn't recommend one without the other. That's why we recommend supplements. It's also an extra stream of income.

Q: What about referral programs?

A: This is one of the programs that I find many hair care professionals overlook.

Referrals tie in with the next subject which is the customer appreciation. The way the referral program works is you tell the customer, 'We are launching a new referral competition program, would you mind giving me a few referrals. Next month we're going to have an awards breakfast, lunch or dinner, as an appreciation. We will have this every month, during this event we reward the participants. We allow all customers to bring as many guests as they like.'

They bring two or three guests and then maybe one of these guests becomes a client.

Then the next month the new client brings two guests and that client gets an award. They get a free breakfast, lunch, or dinner there and you build your clientele.

Invite a guest speaker each month for these events to talk about weight loss, nutrition, or the latest hair trends. You can also ask the audience what topics are of interest.

Q: Would you recommend free clinics?

A: Free clinics are basically good for start-ups or adding a new service to what you already provide. What if you're adding hair loss prevention or trichology to your present practice? In order for you to generate new customers, you can sponsor a free clinic.

You can decide to sponsor a half or full day. You could give a free clinic where you provide free consultations. You let the potential customers know the consultations are valued between $125-$225, but for this limited time you're providing them for free.

What you're doing here is that you're beginning to build yourself a database. It is important to understand that these people are seeking help. The free clinic opens the door for you to provide additional services to them. They have hair and/or scalp problems that you can help solve.

You can also offer other services to them. If they come for the free clinic, you may offer them supplements, CDs, DVDs, books, and other products or services that go along the service. Since you know they're having a particular problem, you can offer suggestions that involve your services.

Q: How important are supplements?

A: Supplements can be something that generate a pretty good income for you, especially if you incorporate the mineral analysis and you find out what the deficiencies or excesses are.

I recommend that anyone considering becoming either a hair loss prevention specialist or a trichologist get a personal mineral analysis for themselves.

Q: How about writing a book, would you recommend that?

A: Writing a book or recommending books that are already written can help generate additional income. If a client has a particular disorder and you know a particular book on the subject recommend it. If you have the book in your place of business, you can sell it to them.

If not, you can always create what we call 'content.' A book is one way to create that kind of content.

Q: How useful are CDs?

A: Actually you can take a book and put it in CD form. You can take a DVD and just take the words off of it and make a CD. You can take that same CD and have it transcribed into a book.

All of them go hand-in-hand in creating different streams of income for yourself and information products for your clients.

Q: How useful are webinars?

A: Webinars are becoming one of the fastest growing ways of getting content from you to the end consumer. The cost of putting together a webinar is reasonable and the return on that investment can be quite lucrative.

You can create a webinar series. You can provide a four-webinars series on nutrition for $29/each or $197/total and have 100 participants. You do the math. You can do the same with weight loss or hair care. There is a high demand for those types of webinars now.

Q: What about teleseminars?

A: Teleseminars are currently more popular than webinars, because more people have phones than internet. However, that's slowly changing, but right now to do a teleseminar tends to be easier and a little less expensive than a webinar.

What we're doing right now could be considered a teleseminar. Get people on the line and it's a done deal. You can do teleseminars at no cost to you. It doesn't cost us anything to provide it, but the participants pay $18.95 to $29.95 to listen to the information.

Q: What about one-on-one coaching?

A: You can charge as much as $1,000 per client for one-on-one coaching. Of course, if you've got 10 clients paying $1,000 a month, that's $10,000 a month. You're pretty well on your way to the $100,000 plus bracket that we talked about.

Q: What about group coaching?

A: You wouldn't charge as much for group coaching as you would for one-on-one coaching. If you get 20 people paying $500 a month, you're still on your way to six figures. These people really need the info you provide with coaching and are happy to pay for it.

Q: What about boot camps?

A: A good place for boot camps are state parks. They're in the middle of nowhere, we're isolated, studying the business of hair and how to generate multiple streams of income.

How do you create a book? How do you create a seminar? How do you create a webinar? We talk about these things in detail.

At the end of this long weekend, you will have your total product. You will have something you can sell.

Q: How important are special reports?

A: Whatever you're doing, you can do a special report on, whether it's color cuts, hair loss, or something else. These special reports are actually given away to build your database.

They're not something that you sell, but you certainly can if you want to. For example, if you go to my website and give me your name and email address, you'll get a special report on this particular subject.

If you're selling your seminar or coaching program, the perceived value should always be 10 times more than they paid for.

In other words, if it's $100 program, then they should pay about $10. If it's a $1,000 program, they should pay $100. If it's a $10,000 program, they should pay $1,000 for it.

Q: How useful is a home study course?

A: This can be a combination of your books, your webinars, your teleseminars, and your coaching programs. Package these things and offer this as a home study course.

Q: What about membership sites?

A: A membership site is a place where members get new information every month. They have continuous access as long as they pay. They can go back and look at previous webinars and seminars to review and every month you're giving them something new and relevant.

They have to be a member to view this site. It's about $49.97 a month or $97 a month or $197 a month. What you charge is up to you. If you get 100, or 1,000 people every month, you're well on your way.

The objective of the multiple streams of income is to produce products and/or services able to create $10,000 plus a month in income.

Q: What about live seminars?

A: People who buy your books and CDs, listen to your teleseminars or watch your webinars are people who also want to see you live. They'll pay $497 or more to see you live.

We want them to be able to understand the fact that there's money to be made on the other side of the chair, that there is life besides just doing hair in our industry.